THE POSITIVITY PROJECT

SIMPLE STEPS TO A MORE FULFILLING LIFE

PRASHANT ZAMBRE

Made with ♥ on the Notion Press Platform
www.notionpress.com

"To all the amazing people out there who believe in the power of positivity and never give up on their dreams. This book is for you, the ones who strive for happiness and fulfillment every day. May these simple steps remind you of the importance of positivity, gratitude, and self-care in creating a more fulfilling life. Let this be a source of inspiration and encouragement as you continue to spread joy and positivity in the world. With love and gratitude."

Contents

Contents

Foreword

"In a world that often seems filled with negativity and stress, it can be easy to lose sight of the importance of positivity and self-care. That's why I am so excited to introduce you to "The Positivity Project." In these pages, you will find simple and practical steps that you can take to cultivate a more positive outlook on life and achieve greater happiness and fulfillment. Whether you're someone who is already well-versed in the power of positivity or just starting out on your journey, this book will serve as a valuable resource. So take a deep breath, open your mind, and get ready to embrace a brighter, more fulfilling future. The power to create a positive life is within you, and "The Positivity Project" is here to help you unleash it."

Foreword

[illegible]

Preface

Welcome to The Positivity Project! In this book, you'll find simple steps to help you create a more fulfilling life and have a positive outlook on life. We'll explore how to be more present in our daily lives, increase our self-awareness and self-care, cultivate healthy relationships, and practice gratitude and mindfulness. We'll also discuss how to stay motivated and focused on our goals, and how to make positive changes in our lives. So let's get started!

Acknowledgements

I would like to express my heartfelt thanks to all those who have made this book possible. First and foremost, I would like to thank my editor and publisher for their guidance and support. I am also grateful to my family, friends, and colleagues for their encouragement and enthusiasm. Last but not least, I am thankful for the countless people who have inspired me to write this book and to share the benefits of positive thinking. Thank you all for your part in bringing The Positivity Project to life.

CHAPTER ONE

Introduction: The Power of Positive Thinking

Have you ever heard the saying, "mind over matter"? This phrase refers to the power of the mind to influence our thoughts, emotions, and actions. In recent years, researchers have been studying the effects of positive thinking on mental and physical health, and the results are compelling. Positive thinking can improve our well-being, reduce stress and anxiety, and even enhance our immune system.

What is Positive Thinking?

Positive thinking is an optimistic mindset that focuses on the good in life, even in the face of adversity. It involves a shift in our attitude and beliefs towards a more hopeful and constructive outlook. Positive thinking does not mean ignoring problems or denying reality; instead, it involves reframing our thoughts and emotions in a more positive light.

The Power of Positive Thinking

The power of positive thinking lies in its ability to influence our perceptions, emotions, and behaviors. Studies have shown that positive thinking can have numerous benefits for our mental and physical health, including:

Improved Mental Health: Positive thinking has been linked to lower rates of depression, anxiety, and stress. It can help us cope with difficult situations, and develop greater resilience to challenges.

Enhanced Physical Health: Positive thinking can also have a positive impact on our physical health. Studies have found that positive emotions can strengthen the immune system, reduce inflammation, and even lower blood pressure.

Greater Success: Positive thinking can improve our self-esteem, motivation, and confidence, leading to greater success in our personal and professional lives.

Improved Relationships: Positive thinking can also improve our relationships with others, by promoting empathy, kindness, and generosity.

How to Cultivate Positive Thinking

Cultivating positive thinking is not always easy, but it is a skill that can be learned and practiced. Some strategies for developing a more positive mindset include:

Gratitude: Practicing gratitude involves focusing on the good things in our lives, and expressing appreciation for them. This can help us cultivate a more positive outlook, and reduce negative thoughts and emotions.

Mindfulness: Mindfulness involves being fully present in the moment, and observing our thoughts and emotions without judgment. This can help us become more aware of our negative thought patterns, and learn to let go of them.

Cognitive Restructuring: Cognitive restructuring involves identifying and challenging negative thought patterns, and replacing them with more positive and realistic thoughts.

Positive Self-Talk: Positive self-talk involves replacing negative self-talk with positive affirmations, which can help us develop a more optimistic and self-assured mindset.

Conclusion

In conclusion, the power of positive thinking lies in its ability to influence our perceptions, emotions, and behaviors. By cultivating a more positive mindset, we can improve our mental and physical health, achieve greater success in our personal and professional lives, and build stronger relationships with others. With practice and persistence, anyone can develop a more positive outlook on life, and reap the benefits of this powerful mindset.

CHAPTER TWO

Understanding Your Thoughts: The First Step to a Positive Mindset

Welcome to Chapter 2 of "The Positivity Project: Simple Steps to a More Fulfilling Life!" In this chapter, we're going to dive into the first step in cultivating a positive mindset: understanding your thoughts.

Have you ever stopped to think about the thoughts that run through your mind each day? For many of us, our thoughts are like a constant stream, flowing endlessly in the background. Some of these thoughts are positive and uplifting, while others are negative and draining. The truth is, the quality of our thoughts has a profound impact on our mental, emotional, and physical well-being.

So, what are your thoughts like? Do you tend to focus on the positive or the negative? Are your thoughts filled with self-doubt, or do you have a strong sense of confidence and self-belief? Understanding the quality of your thoughts is an important first step in cultivating a positive mindset.

Here's a simple exercise to help you get started:

Take a moment to close your eyes and focus inward. Pay attention to the thoughts that are running through your mind. Try to become aware of your thoughts without judgment. Just observe them, and notice the patterns that emerge.

Are your thoughts mostly positive or negative? Are they focused on the past, present, or future? Do you find yourself dwelling on the same negative thoughts over and over again?

Take note of what you discover. This simple exercise can help you to gain a deeper understanding of your thoughts, and can serve as a starting point for developing a more positive mindset.

Now, let's talk about why it's important to pay attention to your thoughts. The truth is, our thoughts shape our reality. Our thoughts influence our attitudes, our behavior, and our perceptions of the world around us. When we think negative thoughts, we're more likely to experience negative emotions, such as anxiety and depression. Conversely, when we focus on positive thoughts, we experience greater happiness and well-being.

So, how do we cultivate a positive mindset? The key is to become more aware of your thoughts, and to actively choose to focus on the positive. This means recognizing and letting go of negative thoughts, and choosing instead to focus on thoughts that are uplifting and supportive.

One of the best ways to do this is to practice gratitude. When we focus on what we're grateful for, we're less likely to dwell on negative thoughts, and more likely to experience positive emotions. You can practice gratitude by keeping a gratitude journal, where you write down three things you're grateful for each day. Or, you can take a few moments each day to reflect on what you're grateful for.

Another way to cultivate a positive mindset is to practice positive affirmations. Positive affirmations are simple, positive statements that help to reinforce a positive outlook. For example, you might say to yourself, "I am worthy and deserving of happiness and success." Repeat your affirmations to yourself regularly, and watch as your thoughts and attitudes begin to shift in a more positive direction.

In conclusion, understanding your thoughts is an important first step in cultivating a positive mindset. By becoming more aware of your thoughts, and actively choosing to focus on the positive, you can experience greater happiness, success, and fulfillment in your life. So, start paying attention to your thoughts today, and get ready to experience the many benefits of a positive outlook!

CHAPTER THREE

The Importance of Gratitude: Fostering a Sense of Appreciation

Welcome to Chapter 3 of "The Positivity Project: Simple Steps to a More Fulfilling Life!" In this chapter, we're going to explore the incredible power of gratitude and how it can help to foster a sense of appreciation in our lives.

Gratitude is a powerful emotion that has the ability to transform our lives in remarkable ways. When we practice gratitude, we focus on the good things in our lives, and we experience a greater sense of happiness and well-being. In fact, studies have shown that people who practice gratitude on a regular basis experience lower levels of stress and depression, and higher levels of happiness and satisfaction.

So, what exactly is gratitude, and how do we practice it? Gratitude is simply a feeling of appreciation for the things in our lives. It can be as simple as being thankful for a warm bed to sleep in at night, or for the love and support of our friends and family.

One of the best ways to practice gratitude is to keep a gratitude journal. Each day, write down three things you're grateful for. They can be big or small, but they should be things that bring a smile to your face and a sense of appreciation to your heart.

Another way to practice gratitude is to take a moment each day to reflect on what you're grateful for. You might choose to meditate, or simply to sit quietly and think about the good things in your life.

It's also helpful to express gratitude to others. When we express gratitude to someone, we're not only reinforcing our own sense of appreciation, but we're also helping to build stronger, more meaningful relationships. So, take the time to write a thank you note to someone who has made a positive impact on your life, or to simply tell someone you appreciate them.

Now, let's talk about why gratitude is so important. When we focus on the things we're grateful for, we're less likely to dwell on negative thoughts and emotions. We're more likely to experience positive emotions, like happiness and contentment, and we're less likely to experience negative emotions like anger and anxiety.

In addition, gratitude has the power to help us see the world in a new light. When we focus on the good things in our lives, we're less likely to take them for granted. We experience a deeper sense of appreciation for the things we have, and we're more likely to see the world in a positive light.

Finally, gratitude has the power to help us build stronger, more meaningful relationships. When we express gratitude to others, we reinforce our bonds and build trust. We show others that we appreciate them, and we create a positive, supportive environment.

In conclusion, gratitude is a powerful emotion that has the ability to transform our lives in remarkable ways. By focusing on the things we're grateful for, we can experience greater happiness, build stronger relationships, and see the world in a positive light. So, start practicing gratitude today, and get ready to experience the many benefits of a thankful heart!

Here are some examples of ways to write gratitude:

Gratitude Journal: Start each day by writing down three things you're grateful for. This could be anything from a good night's sleep, to a supportive friend, to a delicious meal. Writing down your gratitude helps you focus on the good things in your life and encourages you to feel more positive emotions.

Thank You Notes: Express your gratitude to others by writing thank you notes. You can write a note to someone who has made a positive impact on your life, or simply to someone you appreciate. Expressing gratitude to others helps to reinforce your own sense of appreciation, and helps to build stronger, more meaningful relationships.

Gratitude Letters: Write a letter to someone who has made a positive impact on your life, but who you haven't had the chance to thank in person. Express your gratitude and share specific examples of how this person has helped you.

Gratitude List: Write a list of all the things you're grateful for. This could be a list of people, experiences, or simply things that make you happy. Reviewing your gratitude list helps you focus on the positive aspects of your life and encourages you to feel more thankful.

Gratitude Jar: Fill a jar with notes or small tokens that represent things you're grateful for. You could write a note each day, or simply add something to the jar when you feel grateful. Reviewing your gratitude jar helps you focus on the positive aspects of your life and encourages you to feel more thankful.

These are just a few examples of ways to write about gratitude. The key is to find a method that works for you, and to make gratitude a daily habit. When you focus on the things you're grateful for, you'll experience greater happiness, stronger relationships, and a more positive outlook on life!

CHAPTER FOUR

Finding Joy in the Little Things: The Power of Mindfulness

Mindfulness is a powerful tool that can help you find joy and fulfillment in everyday life. It involves paying attention to your thoughts, feelings, and surroundings in a non-judgmental way, and embracing the present moment fully. When you're mindful, you're able to see the beauty and joy in the little things that often go unnoticed, and experience a sense of happiness and contentment.

One of the biggest benefits of mindfulness is that it helps you to find joy in the present moment, rather than constantly searching for happiness in the future. This means that you can experience a sense of joy and contentment simply by taking the time to appreciate the little things in life. Whether it's a warm cup of coffee, a beautiful sunset, or a kind word from a friend, these little moments can bring us a lot of happiness.

The good news is that anyone can cultivate a more mindful and joyful mindset by making a few small changes to their daily routine.

Here are a few tips for finding joy in the little things through mindfulness:

Practice mindfulness regularly: Set aside a few moments each day to focus your attention on the present moment. This could be as simple as taking a few deep breaths, going for a walk, or enjoying a quiet moment of reflection. The key is to make mindfulness a daily habit, so that you can cultivate a more positive and joyful mindset. Consider setting aside a specific time each day for mindfulness, such as first thing in the morning or just before bed. This will help you to establish a routine, and make it easier to incorporate mindfulness into your daily life.

Take notice of your surroundings: Pay attention to your surroundings and take notice of the little things that bring you joy. This could be the sound of birds singing, the scent of flowers, or simply the feeling of the sun on your skin. By focusing your attention on these small moments, you'll be more likely to experience feelings of joy and gratitude. Try to slow down and savor these moments, rather than rushing through them.

Practice gratitude: Take the time each day to reflect on the things you're grateful for. This could be as simple as writing down three things you're thankful for each day, or expressing your gratitude to someone who has made a positive impact on your life. Gratitude helps to reinforce your sense of appreciation, and can help you to find joy in the little things. You might also consider keeping a gratitude journal, where you can write down the things you're thankful for each day. Over time, this can help you to see the positive aspects of your life.

Embrace the present moment: Try to let go of your worries and concerns, and embrace the present moment fully. This means accepting your thoughts and feelings as they are, without judgment, and focusing on the present moment. When you're able to do this, you'll be more likely to experience feelings of joy and peace.

In conclusion, finding joy in the little things is a powerful way to cultivate a more positive and fulfilling life. By practicing mindfulness, taking notice of your surroundings, practicing gratitude, and embracing the present moment, you'll be able to see the beauty and joy in everyday life, and experience a sense of happiness and contentment.

CHAPTER FIVE

Letting Go of Negative Thoughts: The Benefits of Cognitive Restructuring

The human mind is a powerful tool, capable of creating incredible works of art, solving complex problems, and experiencing a range of emotions. Unfortunately, it can also be a source of negativity, self-doubt, and worry. Negative thoughts can have a profound impact on our lives, affecting our moods, behaviors, and relationships. In order to live a happy and fulfilling life, it is essential that we learn to let go of these negative thoughts and embrace positive and constructive thinking. This is where the concept of cognitive restructuring comes in.

Cognitive restructuring is a psychological technique that involves identifying and changing negative thought patterns. This process involves becoming aware of our thoughts and examining them in a critical and objective manner. By doing so, we can challenge the validity of our negative thoughts and replace them with more positive and productive ones.

The benefits of cognitive restructuring are numerous.

Here are a few of the most important:

Improved Mental Health: Negative thoughts can lead to feelings of anxiety, depression, and low self-esteem. By restructuring our thoughts, we can reduce the impact of negative emotions and improve our overall mental health.

Increased Self-Confidence: Negative thoughts can make us feel inadequate, which can lead to decreased self-confidence. By restructuring our thoughts, we can focus on our strengths and abilities, which can lead to increased self-confidence and a more positive self-image.

Better Relationships: Negative thoughts can cause us to view others in a negative light and create unnecessary conflicts in our relationships. By restructuring our thoughts, we can become more empathetic and understanding, leading to stronger and more fulfilling relationships.

Improved Problem-Solving Skills: Negative thoughts can lead us to focus on problems rather than solutions. By restructuring our thoughts, we can approach problems with a more positive and constructive mindset, leading to better problem-solving skills.

Increased Happiness and Satisfaction: Negative thoughts can make us feel unhappy and dissatisfied with life. By restructuring our thoughts, we can focus on the positive aspects of life and experience increased happiness and satisfaction.

Let's dive a bit deeper into the topic of letting go of negative thoughts and the benefits of cognitive restructuring.

One of the main reasons why negative thoughts can be so harmful is because they tend to be self-perpetuating. Once we get into the habit of thinking negatively, it can be difficult to break out of it. This is why cognitive restructuring is such an effective technique. By actively working to change our thought patterns, we can interrupt this cycle and start to see things in a more positive light.

So, what exactly is cognitive restructuring and how does it work? Essentially, it involves becoming more aware of our thoughts and examining them in a critical and objective manner. This means paying attention to the language we use, the tone of our thoughts, and the emotions they evoke. Then, we can start to challenge the validity of these negative thoughts by asking ourselves questions like:

Is this thought really true?

Am I seeing the whole picture or just focusing on one aspect of the situation?

How can I reframe this thought in a more positive and productive way?

By engaging in this process, we can start to replace negative thoughts with positive, constructive ones. This shift in thinking can have a profound impact on our lives in many ways.

For example, improved mental health is a key benefit of cognitive restructuring. Negative thoughts can be incredibly damaging to our mental well-being, causing feelings of anxiety, depression, and low self-esteem. By learning to challenge these thoughts and focus on the positive, we can reduce their impact and improve our overall mental health.

Another benefit of cognitive restructuring is increased self-confidence. When we're stuck in a pattern of negative thinking, it's easy to feel inadequate and uncertain about our abilities. However, by learning to focus on our strengths and accomplishments, we can build a more positive self-image and experience increased self-confidence. This can lead to a greater sense of fulfillment and happiness, as well as better performance in our personal and professional lives.

In addition to these personal benefits, cognitive restructuring can also lead to stronger relationships. When we're mired in negative thoughts, it's easy to view others in a negative light and create unnecessary conflicts. By learning to approach situations with a more positive and understanding mindset, we can become better at seeing things from other people's perspectives and build stronger, more fulfilling relationships.

Lastly, cognitive restructuring can help us become better problem-solvers. When we're stuck in a negative thought pattern, it can be difficult to see things in a constructive manner. We may become overly focused on the problems and obstacles in front of us, rather than finding ways to overcome them. By learning to approach problems with a more positive and productive mindset, we can become more creative and effective problem-solvers.

In conclusion, the benefits of cognitive restructuring are numerous and far-reaching. Whether you're looking to improve your mental health, build self-confidence, strengthen your relationships, or become a better problem-solver, this technique can help. So if you're ready to break free from negative thoughts and embrace a more positive outlook on life, give cognitive restructuring a try! It's a journey that's well worth taking.

CHAPTER SIX

Building Positive Relationships: The Impact of Social Support

Hey there! We all know that having positive relationships is super important for our overall happiness and well-being. As social beings, we naturally crave connection, interaction, and support from others. Positive relationships give us a sense of belonging, security, and provide social support that helps us through tough times. In this chapter, we'll talk about how social support impacts our mental and physical health and share some ways to build positive relationships through social support.

The Impact of Social Support on Mental Health:

Social support has a significant impact on our mental health. Studies have shown that people with strong social support networks tend to have better mental health outcomes than those without support. Social support provides emotional comfort, reduces loneliness and isolation, and helps us feel good about ourselves. When we feel supported, we're better able to deal with stress, trauma, and emotional struggles.

For example, one study found that people who received social support were less likely to develop depression than those who didn't get support. Another study showed that people without social support had a greater risk of experiencing anxiety and depression.

The Impact of Social Support on Physical Health:

Social support is also important for our physical health. Research shows that people with stronger social support networks tend to be healthier than those without support. Social support can provide practical help, like assistance with daily tasks or financial help, which can contribute to better physical health outcomes.

For example, one study found that social support was linked to lower blood pressure in both men and women. Another study showed that people who received social support had a lower risk of getting sick with colds and other illnesses.

Building Positive Relationships through Social Support:

Now, let's talk about some ways to build positive relationships through social support.

Connect with others:

Connecting with others is the first step in building positive relationships. It can be tough to meet new people, but there are many ways to do so, like joining a club or volunteering in your community. When we connect with others, we create opportunities for social support and build a sense of belonging.

Be a good listener:

Being a good listener is a crucial part of social support. When we listen to others, we show that we care and create a safe space for them to share their thoughts and feelings. Active listening involves paying attention, asking questions, and offering empathy and support.

Offer practical support:

Practical support is a tangible way to provide social support. It can include helping with daily tasks, giving rides, or offering financial assistance. Providing practical support can help relieve stress and promote positive relationships.

Offer emotional support:

Emotional support is key to building positive relationships. It involves providing comfort, empathy, and validation to others. You can offer emotional support through words of encouragement, listening, and showing empathy.

Conclusion:

In summary, social support is critical for building positive relationships and promoting mental and physical health. We can build positive relationships through social support by connecting with others, being a good listener, offering practical support, and emotional support. By building positive relationships through social support, we create a sense of belonging, security, and a source of support that helps us get through life's challenges.

CHAPTER SEVEN

EMBRACING FAILURE: TURNING SETBACKS INTO OPPORTUNITIES

Hey there! We all know that failure is a part of life. We all experience setbacks, disappointments, and failures at some point in our lives. But instead of letting failure hold us back, we can choose to embrace it and use it as an opportunity for growth and learning. In this chapter, we'll talk about why embracing failure is important and share some ways to turn setbacks into opportunities.

Why Embracing Failure is Important:

Embracing failure is important because it helps us grow and learn. When we fail, we're forced to confront our mistakes and weaknesses, and this gives us the opportunity to reflect and make changes. Failure can be painful and discouraging, but it can also be a catalyst for personal growth and self-improvement.

For example, think about a time when you failed at something. Maybe it was a job interview, a test, or a relationship. It probably felt terrible at the time, but looking back, you might be able to see how that failure helped you grow and learn. Maybe it taught you to be more prepared, more resilient, or more self-aware. Embracing failure means looking for the lessons in our setbacks and using those lessons to move forward.

Turning Setbacks into Opportunities:

Now, let's talk about some ways to turn setbacks into opportunities.

Reframe your mindset:

The first step to embracing failure is to reframe your mindset. Instead of seeing failure as a negative thing, try to see it as an opportunity for growth and learning. Reframe failure as a natural part of the learning process, rather than a sign of weakness or incompetence.

Learn from your mistakes:

The next step is to learn from your mistakes. Take the time to reflect on what went wrong and what you could do differently next time. Ask yourself what you can learn from the experience and how you can use that knowledge to improve in the future.

Seek feedback:

Seeking feedback is a great way to turn setbacks into opportunities. Ask for feedback from friends, family, or colleagues to gain a different perspective on your failures. Be open to constructive criticism and use it to improve.

Take action:

The final step is to take action. Use what you've learned to make changes and take steps towards your goals. Set new goals and make a plan for how to achieve them. Remember that failure is not the end, it's just a setback on the path to success.

Conclusion:

In summary, embracing failure is an important part of personal growth and self-improvement. By reframing our mindset, learning from our mistakes, seeking feedback, and taking action, we can turn setbacks into opportunities for growth and learning. Remember, failure is not the end, it's just a part of the learning process. So, embrace your failures, learn from them, and use them to move forward and achieve your goals.

CHAPTER EIGHT

Achieving Goals with a Positive Attitude: The Power of Visualization

Hey there! *Do you have big goals you want to achieve, but struggle with staying motivated and positive?* You're not alone! Achieving goals can be tough, and it's easy to get bogged down in negative thoughts and emotions. But there's a powerful tool that can help: ***visualization***. In this chapter, we'll explore the science behind visualization and share some tips on how to use it to achieve your goals with a positive attitude.

The Science of Visualization:

Visualization is a technique that involves creating a mental image or scenario in your mind. When we visualize something, our brain processes that information as if it were real, activating the same neural pathways as if we were actually experiencing the event. This can help us build confidence, reduce anxiety, and improve our performance.

For example, if you want to improve your public speaking skills, you could visualize yourself giving a successful presentation in front of a large audience. By visualizing the scenario, you can create a sense of familiarity and comfort, reducing anxiety and improving your performance.

Tips for Visualization:

Now, let's talk about some tips for using visualization to achieve your goals with a positive attitude.

Start with a clear goal:

The first step to visualization is to have a clear goal in mind.

What do you want to achieve?

Be specific and write down your goal. This will help you create a more detailed mental image when you visualize.

Find a quiet, comfortable place:

To visualize effectively, you need to be in a relaxed and focused state of mind. Find a quiet, comfortable place where you won't be disturbed.

Use all your senses:

When visualizing, it's important to use all your senses. Imagine the scene as vividly as possible, using all your senses.

What does it look like?

What does it feel like?

What sounds can you hear?

The more details you can include, the more effective the visualization will be.

Visualize in the present tense:

When visualizing, it's important to use the present tense. Imagine yourself achieving your goal in the present moment, rather than in the future. This helps create a sense of familiarity and makes the scenario feel more real.

Visualize frequently:

To make visualization effective, you need to do it frequently. Try to visualize your goal every day, even if it's just for a few minutes. This will help reinforce the mental image and make it feel more familiar.

Benefits of Visualization:

So, *why is visualization so powerful?*

Here are some benefits:

Increased motivation:

Visualization can help increase motivation by creating a sense of excitement and anticipation around your goal. When you can vividly imagine yourself achieving your goal, it can help you stay motivated and focused.

Improved performance:

Visualizing success can improve performance by reducing anxiety and increasing confidence. By imagining yourself performing well, you can create a sense of familiarity and comfort, making it easier to perform at your best.

Positive attitude:

Visualization can help cultivate a positive attitude by focusing on the positive aspects of your goal. When you imagine yourself succeeding, it can create a sense of optimism and positivity.

Conclusion:

In summary, visualization is a powerful tool for achieving your goals with a positive attitude. By creating a mental image of your goal, using all your senses, and visualizing frequently, you can increase motivation, improve performance, and cultivate a positive attitude. Remember, visualization is not a magic solution, but it can be a helpful tool to keep you focused and motivated on your journey towards achieving your goals. So, keep visualizing, stay positive, and keep moving forward!

CHAPTER NINE

The Benefits of Physical Exercise: Improving Mental and Emotional Well-being

Hello! *Are you looking for a way to improve your mental and emotional well-being?* If so, physical exercise might be the answer. Exercise is often associated with physical health, but it also has significant benefits for our mental and emotional well-being. In this chapter, we'll explore the science behind these benefits and share some tips on how to incorporate exercise into your daily routine.

The Science of Exercise and Mental Health:

Research shows that exercise has a profound impact on our mental and emotional well-being. Here are some of the key ways that exercise can improve our mental health:

Reducing stress and anxiety:

Exercise can help reduce stress and anxiety by releasing endorphins, which are chemicals that improve our mood and reduce feelings of stress and anxiety.

Improving mood and self-esteem:

Physical exercise has been shown to improve our mood and increase self-esteem. Exercise can help us feel more confident and in control, which can have a positive impact on our mental and emotional well-being.

Boosting cognitive function:

Exercise has been linked to improved cognitive function, including better memory, attention, and problem-solving skills. This can help us feel more focused and productive in our daily lives.

Reducing symptoms of depression:

Regular exercise has been shown to reduce symptoms of depression, including low mood, lack of energy, and feelings of hopelessness.

Tips for Incorporating Exercise into Your Routine:

Now that we know about the benefits of exercise, let's talk about some tips for incorporating it into our daily routine.

Start small:

If you're new to exercise, start small and gradually increase your activity level over time. Begin with 10-15 minutes of activity each day and work your way up to 30 minutes or more.

Find an activity you enjoy:

It's important to find an exercise activity that you enjoy, as this will help you stick to it long-term. Whether it's walking, jogging, swimming, or yoga, find an activity that you enjoy and that fits into your schedule.

Make it a priority:

Schedule exercise into your daily routine and make it a priority. Treat it like any other important appointment and make sure to stick to it.

Mix it up:

Variety is key when it comes to exercise. Mix up your routine by trying different activities or adding new challenges to your existing routine.

Set realistic goals:

Set realistic goals for your exercise routine, and celebrate your progress along the way. This will help keep you motivated and focused on your long-term goals.

Conclusion:

In conclusion, physical exercise is a powerful tool for improving our mental and emotional well-being. By reducing stress and anxiety, improving mood and self-esteem, boosting cognitive function, and reducing symptoms of depression, exercise has a profound impact on our mental health. By incorporating exercise into our daily routine, we can experience these benefits and improve our overall well-being. So, start small, find an activity you enjoy, make it a priority, mix it up, and set realistic goals. With these tips in mind, you'll be on your way to a happier, healthier you!

CHAPTER TEN

Giving Back: The Power of Altruism in Building Positivity

Hello! *Do you ever feel like you want to make a positive impact in the world?* One of the most effective ways to do this is through acts of altruism, or selfless acts of kindness towards others. In this chapter, we'll explore the power of altruism in building positivity and share some tips on how to incorporate giving back into your daily life.

The Science of Altruism:

Research shows that altruism has a profound impact on our well-being, both mentally and physically. Here are some of the key ways that altruism can improve our overall positivity:

Boosting happiness and well-being:

Acts of kindness and generosity have been shown to boost happiness and well-being. Giving to others can create a sense of purpose and fulfillment that contributes to a positive outlook on life.

Reducing stress and anxiety:

Helping others has been linked to reduced levels of stress and anxiety. By focusing on the needs of others, we are able to take a step back from our own worries and concerns.

Improving physical health:

Altruism has been linked to improved physical health, including lower blood pressure and reduced risk of chronic diseases.

Strengthening relationships:

Giving back can also strengthen our relationships with others. By helping others, we build connections and create a sense of community.

Tips for Incorporating Altruism into Your Routine:

Now that we know about the benefits of giving back, let's talk about some tips for incorporating altruism into our daily routine.

Find a cause that you care about:

Identify a cause or organization that you are passionate about. Whether it's volunteering at a local shelter, donating to a charity, or simply spreading kindness to those around you, find a way to give back that aligns with your values.

Start small:

You don't need to make grand gestures to give back. Start small by holding the door open for someone, leaving a positive note for a co-worker, or making a small donation to a charity. Every act of kindness counts!

Make it a habit:

Incorporate acts of altruism into your daily routine. Set a goal to do one kind thing for someone else each day, and make it a habit to look for opportunities to help others.

Get involved in your community:

Volunteer in your local community and get involved in local events. This is a great way to build connections and create a sense of belonging while making a positive impact.

Practice gratitude:

Take time to appreciate the things that you have in your life and express gratitude for the opportunities you have to give back. This will help cultivate a positive mindset and reinforce the importance of altruism in your life.

Conclusion:

In conclusion, altruism is a powerful tool for building positivity and improving our overall well-being. By boosting happiness and well-being, reducing stress and anxiety, improving physical health, and strengthening relationships, acts of kindness have a profound impact on our lives. By finding a cause that you care about, starting small, making it a habit, getting involved in your community, and practicing gratitude, you can incorporate altruism into your daily routine and make a positive impact in the world. So, go out there and spread kindness wherever you can, and see the positivity it brings to your life!

CHAPTER ELEVEN

The Importance of Sleep: Recharging the Mind and Body

Hello! *Are you someone who regularly sacrifices sleep in order to get things done?* While it may seem like a good idea in the short term, the long-term effects of sleep deprivation can be detrimental to both our mental and physical health. In this chapter, we'll explore the importance of sleep and the benefits of getting enough rest for our mind and body.

Why Sleep is Important:

Sleep is essential for our bodies and minds to function at their best. Here are some of the key reasons why getting enough sleep is so important:

Restoration:

While we sleep, our bodies undergo essential restorative processes. During this time, our cells and tissues are repaired, and our organs are replenished.

Memory consolidation:

Sleep plays a crucial role in memory consolidation, which is the process by which our brains store and organize new information.

Emotional regulation:

Getting enough sleep is important for regulating our emotions. When we're well-rested, we're better able to handle stress and regulate our mood.

Physical health:

Sleep has a profound impact on our physical health. Research has shown that getting enough sleep can help lower the risk of obesity, diabetes, heart disease, and other chronic illnesses.

The Effects of Sleep Deprivation:

On the other hand, sleep deprivation can have negative effects on our mental and physical health. Here are some of the ways that lack of sleep can impact our lives:

Cognitive impairment:

Sleep deprivation can lead to cognitive impairment, including decreased attention and memory retention.

Emotional instability:

Lack of sleep can also lead to increased emotional instability, making it harder to regulate our emotions and handle stress.

Physical health issues:

Sleep deprivation has been linked to a variety of physical health issues, including obesity, diabetes, and heart disease.

Tips for Getting Better Sleep:

Now that we know the importance of getting enough sleep, let's talk about some tips for improving our sleep habits.

Stick to a sleep schedule:

Try to stick to a regular sleep schedule, going to bed and waking up at the same time each day. This can help regulate our body's natural sleep-wake cycle.

Create a sleep-friendly environment:

Make sure your bedroom is a comfortable and quiet space that is conducive to sleep. Keep the room cool and dark, and avoid using electronics in bed.

Limit caffeine and alcohol:

Caffeine and alcohol can interfere with our sleep, so try to limit these substances, especially in the hours leading up to bedtime.

Relax before bed:

Try to unwind before bed by engaging in relaxing activities, such as reading, listening to calming music, or taking a warm bath.

Exercise regularly:

Regular exercise can help promote better sleep. Just be sure to avoid working out too close to bedtime, as this can interfere with our ability to fall asleep.

Conclusion:

In conclusion, sleep is essential for our overall well-being. Getting enough rest helps restore our bodies and minds, aids in memory consolidation and emotional regulation, and improves our physical health. On the other hand, sleep deprivation can have negative effects on our cognitive and emotional abilities, as well as our physical health. By sticking to a sleep schedule, creating a sleep-friendly environment, limiting caffeine and alcohol, relaxing before bed, and exercising regularly, we can improve our sleep habits and reap the benefits of a well-rested mind and body. So, make sure to prioritize your sleep, and see how it positively impacts your life!

CHAPTER TWELVE

Cultivating a Positive Mindset: A Journey to a More Fulfilling Life.

Do you ever feel like you're stuck in a negative thought cycle, where every little setback feels like a major blow? It's easy to get caught up in negative thinking, but cultivating a positive mindset can have a profound impact on our lives. In this chapter, we'll explore the benefits of having a positive mindset, and provide tips on how to cultivate positivity in your life.

The Power of a Positive Mindset:

Having a positive mindset can benefit us in a number of ways, including:

Improved mental and physical health:

Research has shown that a positive outlook can lead to improved mental and physical health, including lower rates of depression, anxiety, and stress.

Better relationships:

A positive mindset can also lead to more positive interactions with others, leading to better relationships.

Increased resilience:

When we have a positive mindset, we're better equipped to handle setbacks and bounce back from adversity.

Greater success:

Having a positive outlook can help us stay motivated and focused on our goals, leading to greater success in all areas of our lives.

Tips for Cultivating a Positive Mindset:

Now that we know the benefits of a positive mindset, let's talk about some tips for cultivating positivity in our lives:

Practice gratitude:

Take time each day to focus on the things you're grateful for. This can be as simple as jotting down a few things in a gratitude journal, or taking a few minutes to reflect on what you appreciate in your life.

Focus on the positive:

When faced with a setback or negative situation, try to focus on the positive aspects of the situation. Ask yourself what you can learn from the experience, and what opportunities it presents.

Surround yourself with positivity:

Surrounding yourself with positive people and positive environments can help boost your own positivity. Seek out friends who are supportive and uplifting, and spend time in environments that make you feel good.

Practice positive self-talk:

The way we talk to ourselves can have a big impact on our mindset. Try to replace negative self-talk with positive affirmations.

Instead of saying *"I'm not good enough,"* try saying *"I'm capable and strong."*

Practice mindfulness:

Practicing mindfulness can help us stay present in the moment, and avoid getting caught up in negative thoughts. Try incorporating mindfulness practices like meditation or deep breathing into your daily routine.

Conclusion:

Cultivating a positive mindset can have a profound impact on our lives. A positive outlook can lead to improved mental and physical health, better relationships, increased resilience, and greater success. By practicing gratitude, focusing on the positive, surrounding yourself with positivity, practicing positive self-talk, and practicing mindfulness, you can start to cultivate positivity in your life. It's important to remember that cultivating a positive mindset is a journey, and it's okay to have setbacks along the way. The key is to keep working on it, and to keep striving for a more positive and fulfilling life. So, start today and see how cultivating a positive mindset can transform your life!

CHAPTER THIRTEEN

Quotes on Positivity

Reading and reflecting on positive quotes can help you stay positive by providing inspiration, motivation, and encouragement. When you're feeling down or facing a challenge, positive quotes can offer a fresh perspective and remind you to focus on the good in your life. They can also serve as a helpful reminder to practice gratitude and maintain a positive mindset.

Additionally, positive quotes can serve as a form of self-talk. By reading and repeating positive quotes to yourself, you can reinforce positive beliefs and attitudes, and counteract negative self-talk. This can help you build a more positive outlook on life and improve your overall well-being.

So, making a habit of regularly reading and reflecting on positive quotes can help you stay positive, even in the face of challenges or adversity. It can also help you cultivate a more optimistic and resilient mindset, which can lead to greater success and fulfillment in all areas of your life.

"Positivity is the key to a happy and fulfilling life." – Unknown

"Positive anything is better than negative nothing." – Elbert Hubbard

"Positivity is not about ignoring problems, it's about focusing on solutions." – Unknown

"Optimism is a happiness magnet. If you stay positive, good things and good people will be drawn to you." – Mary Lou Retton

"The power of positivity is in its ability to transform our mindset and our reality." – Unknown

"Being positive doesn't mean ignoring the negative. It means overcoming the negative with the power of our thoughts and actions." – Unknown

"A positive attitude can turn a negative situation into a positive one." – Unknown

"The greatest weapon against stress is our ability to choose one thought over another." – William James

"Your attitude determines your altitude." – Zig Ziglar

"Positivity is not just a state of mind, it's a way of life." – Unknown

"Positive thinking is more than just a tagline. It changes the way we behave." – Harvey Mackay

"The more positive your attitude, the more positive your life will become." – Unknown

"Positivity is contagious. Spread it wherever you go." – Unknown

"Positive thoughts breed positive results." – Maria V. Snyder

"Positivity is the fuel that ignites our dreams and propels us towards success." – Unknown

"Believe you can and you're halfway there." – Theodore Roosevelt

"The only limit to our realization of tomorrow will be our doubts of today." – Franklin D. Roosevelt

"Positive thoughts lead to positive actions, which lead to positive results." – Wade Boggs

"The only way to do great work is to love what you do." – Steve Jobs

"A positive attitude gives you power over your circumstances instead of your circumstances having power over you." – Joyce Meyer

"The more positive your thoughts, the more positive your life will be." – Unknown

"Positivity is not just a mindset, it's a way of living life to the fullest." – Unknown

"Positive thinking is the foundation of a happy and fulfilling life." – Unknown

"Positivity is the gateway to a life of abundance, joy, and success." – Unknown

"The key to happiness is a positive mindset and a grateful heart." – Unknown

"Positivity is not just about what you think, it's also about what you do." – Unknown

"Positivity is the seed that grows into a life of happiness, success, and fulfillment." – Unknown

"The more positive your thoughts, the more positive your life will be." – Unknown

"Positivity is not about ignoring the negative, it's about choosing to focus on the positive." – Unknown

"Positive thinking is the pathway to a life of abundance and happiness." – Unknown

Conclusion

In conclusion, The Positivity Project offers a comprehensive and practical guide to developing a positive mindset and living a more fulfilling life. Each chapter highlights a specific aspect of positivity, from understanding your thoughts and fostering gratitude to building positive relationships and embracing failure. The book emphasizes the importance of mindfulness, cognitive restructuring, visualization, physical exercise, and sleep in promoting mental and emotional well-being.

The Power of Positive Thinking is a powerful tool that can help individuals to cultivate a more optimistic and resilient mindset, leading to greater success and fulfillment in all areas of life. By understanding the impact of our thoughts and emotions on our mental and physical health, we can develop strategies to let go of negative thoughts, embrace failure as an opportunity, and build positive relationships. The book also emphasizes the importance of giving back and cultivating altruism, which not only benefits others but also brings a sense of purpose and fulfillment to our own lives.

In short, The Positivity Project offers a roadmap for cultivating a positive mindset, building resilience, and living a more fulfilling life. Whether you are facing challenges in your personal or professional life, this book provides practical tools and techniques to help you stay positive, overcome obstacles, and achieve your goals. With its emphasis on mindfulness, gratitude, and positive relationships, The Positivity Project is a valuable resource for anyone seeking to live a happier, more meaningful life.

9 798889 754602

Printed by Libri Plureos GmbH in Hamburg,
Germany